SCHOLASTIC

Great Grammar Practice

Linda Ward Beech

New York • Toronto • London • Auckland • Sydney
New Delhi • Mexico City • Hong Kong • Buenos Aires

Teaching *Resources*

Edited by Mela Ottaiano
Cover design by Michelle Kim
Interior design by Melinda Belter

ISBN: 978-0-545-79423-7
Copyright © 2015 by Scholastic Inc.
Illustrations copyright © by Scholastic Inc.
All rights reserved.
Published by Scholastic Inc.
Printed in the U.S.A.

2 3 4 5 6 7 8 9 10   40   22 21 20 19 18 17 16

Contents

Introduction

To be successful at any task, it is important to have the right tools and skills. Grammar is one of the basic tools of written and oral language. Students need to learn and practice key grammar skills to communicate effectively. The pages in this book provide opportunities to introduce grammar rules and concepts and/or expand students' familiarity with them.

Using This Book

If your class has grammar texts, you can duplicate the pages in this book to use as reinforcements.

✐ Read aloud the instructions and examples as most of the material will be new to third graders. If necessary, provide additional examples and answer students' questions.

✐ Model how to do the activity.

You can add these pages as assignments to your writing program and keep copies in skills folders at your writing resource center.

You may also want to use the activities as a class lesson or have students complete the pages in small groups.

Page by Page

You can use these suggestions to help students complete the activity pages.

Activity 1
Remind students that statements end with periods and questions end with question marks.

Activity 2
Tell students that most subjects are nouns. Point out *Mimi* and *batter* in the example. Mention that noun markers, such as the article *the* in the example, are part of the subject.

Activity 3
Review what students know about sentence subjects and point out that the main word in a predicate is the verb.

Activity 4
For Part A, remind students that if a sentence begins with a verb, it is a command.

Activity 5
Use this activity to review what students have learned in the previous lessons.

Activity 6
Remind students that a sentence always begins with a capital letter.

Activity 7
Point out that more than one conjunction may make sense in a given sentence.

Activity 8
Stress that the use of one of these subordinating conjunctions signals that a dependent clause is coming. Remind students that a dependent clause is not a complete sentence.

Activity 9
Point out that when the word *since* is used as a conjunction, it is a synonym for *because*.

Activity 10
Review what students know about subjects and predicates. If necessary, review the characteristics of the four sentence types.

Activity 11
Review what students already know about nouns. Help students understand that the nouns they circle in Part A name a person, place, or thing.

Activity 12
In addition to the examples given, review other words that are proper nouns, such as months, days of week, states, holidays, etc.

Activity 13
Introduce the term *abstract* when discussing the nouns on this page. If students have trouble grasping the concept of these nouns, suggest they decide whether a noun can be explicitly pictured—as, for example, a dog or an apple can be.

Activities 14 and 15
Review the terms *singular* and *plural*.

Activity 16
The placement of the apostrophe in possessives is often confusing to students; they may need additional practice.

Activity 17
Review what students already know about pronouns. Point out that the use of pronouns keeps sentences from becoming monotonous. Demonstrate by reading aloud the example sentences, substituting the nouns for the pronouns.

Activities 18 and 19
The misuse of pronouns is a common mistake. Give examples of the misuse of subject pronouns after action verbs such as "You sent we a photo" and the misuse of object pronouns as subjects such as "Him goes for a ride."

Activity 20
Stress that an apostrophe is used where letters are omitted.

Activity 21
Review the purposes of a noun and a pronoun. Remind students that the pronoun must agree with the noun it replaces.

Activity 22
Review what students already know about verbs. Explain that the verb is the main word in a predicate; it is called the simple predicate. Usually, there are other words in a predicate as well.

Activity 23
Noun-verb agreement can be tricky for students. You might do this page aloud with the class so that students can hear the correct usage and talk about why the verb is singular or plural in each sentence.

Activities 24 and 25
Discuss why verb tense is important.

Activity 26
Encourage students to use the chart as they complete this page. You might do this page aloud with the class so that students can hear the correct usage and talk about why the verb is correctly used in each sentence.

Activity 27
Review the terms *syllable*, *consonant*, and *vowel* before introducing this page. Have students tell which rule applies as they complete the exercises.

Activities 28 and 29
Tell students that they should memorize the past tense of these verbs.

 Great Grammar Practice, Grade 3 © 2015 by Scholastic Teaching Resources

Activity 30
Encourage students to think of other verbs that might correctly complete the sentences.

Activity 31
Review what students already know about adjectives and introduce the word *modify*.

Activities 32 and 33
Introduce the terms *comparative* and *superlative* when discussing these activities.

Activity 34
Have students note which spelling rule they use when completing the chart.

Activity 35
Review what students already know about adverbs. Point out that adverbs aren't always next to the verbs they describe.

Activity 36
Explain that adverbs help make the meaning of a sentence clearer, and often more colorful.

Activities 37 and 38
Reintroduce the terms *comparative* and *superlative* when discussing these pages.

Activity 39
Invite volunteers to create a sentence that includes one of the adverbs in the word bank.

Activity 40
Remind students that adverbs aren't always next to the verbs they describe.

Activities 41–43
Explain that prepositions and the phrases they introduce help make a sentence more interesting and informative.

Activity 44
Point out that small words such as *in* and *to* are not capitalized unless they are the first word in a title. Before students begin Part B, remind them that names of people are capitalized.

Activity 45
Before students begin Part B, remind them that sentences begin with capital letters and end with punctuation. Point out that the names of months are capitalized. Remind students that book titles are underlined.

Activity 46
Explain that state abbreviations are almost always used on addresses for letters, packages, and online forms.

Activity 47
Remind students that a comma is like a yellow traffic light for readers; it indicates a slight pause. When used in a series, commas help readers differentiate the items mentioned. Point out that a series must include at least three words or phrases.

Activity 48
Tell students that quotation marks are a form of punctuation. Suggest that students read all of the sentences in speech balloons first before they add them to the sentences in the activity.

Activity 49
After students complete this page, you may wish to go over it aloud with the class so you can discuss the capitalization and punctuation.

Activity 50
Review what students know about capitalizing the first word of a sentence and proper nouns. You may want to point out the abbreviation for *Saint* in sentence 3. If necessary, mention that abbreviations such as this one end in a period.

Activity 51
This page also helps develop vocabulary and dictionary skills. Encourage students to make charts or keep notebooks of word families.

Activity 52

Encourage students to find other words that begin or end with these digraphs.

Activities 53 and 54

Invite students to find other words that begin with these prefixes or end with these suffixes.

Activity 55

Ask volunteers to share other words they may know that begin or end with the given digraphs, prefixes, and suffixes. Point out that there may be more than one way to complete the sentences.

Connections to the Standards

With the goal of providing students nationwide with a quality education that prepares them for college and careers, broad standards were developed to establish rigorous educational expectations. These standards serve as the basis of many state standards. The chart below details how the activities in this book align with specific language and foundational skills standards for students in grade 3.

	English Language Arts Standards	Activities
Language	**Conventions of Standard English**	
	• Demonstrate command of the conventions of standard English grammar and usage when writing or speaking.	1–55
	• Demonstrate command of the conventions of standard English capitalization, punctuation, and spelling when writing.	6, 12–16, 20, 23–25, 27, 32–34, 36–39, 44–55
	Knowledge of Language	
	• Use knowledge of language and its conventions when writing, speaking, reading, or listening.	1–55
	Vocabulary Acquisition and Use	
	• Determine or clarify the meaning of unknown and multiple-meaning words and phrases based on grade 3 reading and content, choosing flexibly from an array of strategies.	1–3, 7, 9, 11, 13, 19–21, 23, 26, 30, 33, 38–40, 42, 43, 48, 51, 53–55
	• Demonstrate understanding of word relationships and nuances in word meanings.	1–55
	• Acquire and use accurately grade-appropriate conversational, general academic, and domain-specific words and phrases, including those that signal spatial and temporal relationships.	1–55
Foundational Skills	**Phonics and Word Recognition**	
	• Know and apply grade-level phonics and word analysis skills in decoding words.	13–16, 23–25, 27–29, 32–39, 53–55
	Fluency	
	• Read with sufficient accuracy and fluency to support comprehension.	1–55

Name _____ Date _____

Two Kinds of Sentences

A sentence is a group of words that expresses a complete idea.

A statement is a sentence that tells something.

A question is a sentence that asks something.

Statement: Our school fair is today.

Question: When is our school fair?

A. Read each sentence. Write *statement* or *question*.

1. Our class is in charge of the crafts booth. _____

2. The fourth graders made posters. _____

3. What time does the fair start? _____

4. The fifth graders are selling food. _____

5. What are the first graders doing? _____

6. Will families come to the fair? _____

7. Some booths will have games. _____

8. Mr. Rice will perform magic tricks. _____

B. Complete the statement and question.

9. The third grade _____ .

10. What prizes _____ ?

Name _____ Date _____

Sentence Subjects

> A sentence has two parts.
> The subject of a sentence tells who or what does something.
>
> **Mini** stirred the batter. **The batter** splashed all over.
>
>
> subject   subject

A. Write the subject of each sentence.

   1. Mini made a sticky mess on the table. _____

   2. The spoon fell out of her hand. _____

   3. The table had batter all over it. _____

   4. Dad added eggs to the bowl. _____

   5. The cake was for Mini's mom. _____

   6. Mom loves chocolate birthday cake! _____

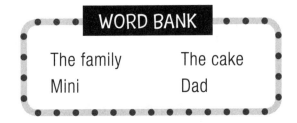

WORD BANK

The family	The cake
Mini	Dad

B. Choose the best subject from the word bank to complete each sentence.

   7. _____ went in the oven to bake.

   8. _____ made some vanilla icing.

   9. _____ helped Dad clean up the kitchen.

  10. _____ enjoyed the delicious birthday cake.

   Great Grammar Practice, Grade 3 © 2015 by Scholastic Teaching Resources

Sentence Predicates

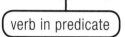

A sentence has two parts.

The predicate of a sentence includes a verb that tells what the subject does.

Sara **rides** her bike after school. Ken **joins** her on his scooter.

↑ verb in predicate   ↑ verb in predicate

A. Circle the subject of each sentence. Write the verb from the predicate.

1. Sara wears a helmet for her bike rides. _____

2. A bike has a seat and pedals. _____

3. A scooter lacks a seat and pedals. _____

4. Ken pushes on the ground with one foot. _____

5. The friends race around their neighborhood. _____

6. They meet other kids in the park. _____

WORD BANK

looks at his watch   ride on bike paths

rings her bell   calls to Sara

B. Choose the best predicate from the word bank to complete each sentence.

7. The kids _____ .

8. Sara _____ .

9. Ken _____ .

10. He _____ .

Name _____ Date _____

More Sentences

A command is a sentence that tells what to do.

The subject of a command is *you*, but it is not said or written.

A command starts with a verb.

Command: Stop right here.

(subject *you* not stated) (command starts with verb)

An exclamation is a sentence that shows strong feeling.

Exclamation: What a surprise!

A. Read each sentence. Write *statement* or *command*.

1. Signs give drivers helpful information. _____

2. Follow the exit signs. _____

3. Turn right at the corner. _____

4. Obey the signs for pedestrians. _____

5. Caution signs offer good advice to drivers. _____

B. Read each sentence. Write *command* or *exclamation*.

6. Slow down! _____

7. Please drive slowly through the park. _____

8. Watch for animals. _____

9. What a shock to see a bear! _____

10. Keep out of this area. _____

Name _____ Date _____

Identifying Sentences

Statements, questions, commands, and exclamations
are different kinds of sentences.

Kind of Sentence	Example
Statement	A vole lives in our garden.
Question	What is a vole?
Command	Look it up on the Internet.
Exclamation	Wow!

Read each sentence. Write *statement*, *question*,
command, or *exclamation*.

1. The vole ran across the patio. _____

2. When did you first see it? _____

3. Jan was leaning over to water some pots. _____

4. What a surprise she had! _____

5. Tell me more about the vole. _____

6. A vole is a small rodent that looks like a mouse. _____

7. How interesting! _____

8. Is a vole related to a mole? _____

9. Why don't we look up voles in a reference book? _____

10. Make some notes about voles for us. _____

Name _____ Date _____

Writing Sentences

A sentence always begins with a capital letter.
Sentences have punctuation at the end.

Kind of Sentence	End Punctuation	Example
Statement	period **.**	Mrs. Hill handed out our papers.
Question	question mark **?**	Were they test papers?
Command	period **.** or exclamation mark **!**	Tell me about them.
Exclamation	exclamation mark **!**	Good work!

Rewrite each sentence so that it is correct.

1. jeb studied hard for the test

_____

2. was he well prepared for all the questions

_____

3. look at his grade

_____

4. fantastic

_____

5. keep up the good work

_____

6. jeb, what is your favorite subject

_____

 Great Grammar Practice, Grade 3 © 2015 by Scholastic Teaching Resources

Name _____ Date _____

Two Ideas

The words *and*, *but*, and *or* can link two ideas in a sentence.

These words are called conjunctions.

Conjunction	Purpose	Example
and	connects two related ideas	It is spring, and some robins are building a nest.
but	ideas that differ or shows a problem with first idea	We like birds, but they make a lot of noise in the morning.
or	suggests a choice of ideas	We can close the window, or we can listen to the noise.

Add *and*, *but*, or *or* to each sentence.

1. The birds worked hard on the nest, _____ it is messy.

2. The female sits on the nest, _____ the male brings her food.

3. Is that bird a robin, _____ is it a swallow?

4. We have a birdhouse on the fence, _____ I haven't seen a bird there.

5. Will the eggs hatch today, _____ will they hatch tomorrow?

6. The baby birds are hungry, _____ their parents feed them.

7. Dad tried to take photos, _____ the birds moved.

8. A bird sat on the wall, _____ dad got a good picture.

9. We can send this photo to Grandpa, _____ we can send that one.

Name _____ Date _____

Clauses in Sentences

A dependent clause is a sentence part. It has a subject and a predicate, but it is not a sentence by itself. Dependent clauses begin with a conjunction.

Dependent Clause Conjunctions

while	although	until	than
because	since	after	before

Sentence: The carpenter hummed softly **while** he worked.

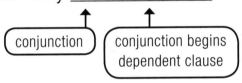

conjunction   conjunction begins dependent clause

A. Circle the conjunction in each sentence. Underline the dependent clause.

1. We studied at the table before it broke.

2. The problem started because Luna ran into the table.

3. The table became wobbly after Luna had this accident.

4. We needed a carpenter because we used the table a lot.

5. We called Jason since he is a good worker.

B. Write *sentence* or *dependent clause* for each group of words.

6. Before the pieces became loose. _____

7. We didn't use the table until it was fixed. _____

8. Although she was very sorry. _____

9. Than buy a new one. _____

10. Jason smiled after he finished the job. _____

Using Conjunctions With Clauses

Some conjunctions begin sentence parts called dependent clauses. A dependent clause has a subject and a predicate, but it is not a sentence by itself.

Sentence: We went to the auditorium **because** there was a talent show.

conjunction   conjunction begins
                       dependent clause

Choose the best conjunction from the word bank to complete the dependent clause in each sentence. Use each word only once.

WORD BANK

after	although	because	before
since	than	until	while

1. Performers waited backstage _____ people took their seats.

2. The audience went silent _____ the lights went down.

3. There were wonderful dancers and actors, _____ I liked the singers the best.

4. Everyone clapped _____ the performances were great!

5. We laughed at each joke _____ they were funny.

6. The show was over _____ we wanted it to end.

7. We can't wait _____ next year's show is ready.

8. I'd rather be in the talent show _____ in the audience!

Name _____ Date _____

Review: Sentences

A sentence is a group of words that expresses a complete idea.

A sentence has two parts: a subject and a predicate.

Statements, questions, commands, and exclamations are different kinds of sentences.

A. Read the sentences. Write the sentence type on the line.

1. We will take the train. _____

2. When do we need to leave? _____

3. Get ready now. _____

4. I love to ride the train! _____

5. Where are we going? _____

B. Circle the complete subject and underline the complete predicate in each sentence.

6. Our grandmother meets us every Sunday.

7. She likes to take us to the museum.

8. My sister and I enjoy looking at paintings.

9. We paint our own pictures when we get home.

10. Grandma thinks we are great artists!

Name _____ Date _____

What Is a Noun?

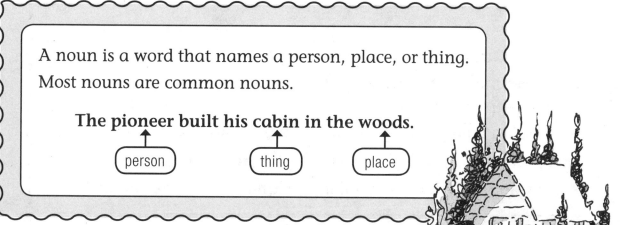

A noun is a word that names a person, place, or thing. Most nouns are common nouns.

The pioneer built his cabin in the woods.

person   thing   place

A. Circle every noun in each sentence.

1. Many trees surrounded the small house.

2. Squirrels, chipmunks, and other animals lived in the forest, too.

3. One day a bear appeared in the clearing around the cabin.

4. The family watched him from a window.

5. The pioneer was glad when this neighbor lumbered away.

B. Add nouns to the blanks in each sentence.

6. The _____ and his _____ cut down some

_____ .

7. They planned to make a _____ for the _____ .

8. Some _____ from the nearby _____ came to help.

9. The _____ cooked a big _____ for the

_____ .

10. Everyone worked hard and had a good _____ .

Name _____ Date _____

Proper Nouns

Most nouns are common nouns.

Nouns that name a particular person, place, or thing are proper nouns.

Each word in a proper noun begins with a capital letter.

Common nouns:	city	girl	country	court
Proper nouns:	Atlanta	Ellen	Canada	Supreme Court

A. Underline the common nouns in each sentence. Circle the proper nouns.

1. Peter and his friends ate dinner together on Tuesday.

2. The group went to the First Wok on Mulberry Street.

3. Jodi knew the chef at this restaurant.

4. Hector and Anna caught the train at Falls Village.

5. They passed the Mountain View School on their way to the station.

B. Decide if each word is a common noun or a proper noun.
Write *common noun* or rewrite each proper noun correctly.

6. lake erie _____

7. highway _____

8. flag day _____

9. europe _____

10. library _____

11. sunday _____

12. month _____

Name _____ Date _____

Other Kinds of Nouns

Some nouns name ideas, qualities, or feelings.
These nouns name things that cannot be seen or touched.

Abstract Nouns

fear	love	anger	honesty	peace	loyalty
curiosity	hate	pleasure	justice	liberty	truth

Some abstract nouns are formed by adding *-hood, -ment,*
or *-ness* to other words.

child + hood = childhood   **enjoy + ment = enjoyment**
kind + ness = kindness

A. Write the noun from each sentence that names an idea, quality, or feeling.

1. Nan showed her contentment with a smile.   _____

2. The concert provided real pleasure.   _____

3. The audience liked the pureness of the music.   _____

4. Many people discovered a new love for music.   _____

5. The music made Eli think of brotherhood.   _____

6. He liked the gentleness of what he heard.   _____

7. He marveled at its beauty.   _____

8. It gave him great joy.   _____

B. Write two sentences using an abstract noun from the examples in the chart above.

9. _____

10. _____

Plural Nouns

Plural nouns name more than one person, place, or thing.

Most plural nouns end in *-s* or *-es*.

Singular nouns that end in *ch*, *sh*, *x*, *s*, or *ss* end in *-es* in their plural form.

Singular Nouns	Plural Nouns
flower	flowers
lunch	lunches
dash	dashes
fox	foxes
walrus	walruses
class	classes

A. Write the plural for each noun.

1. brush _____
2. pass _____
3. bunch _____
4. fax _____
5. guess _____

6. plant _____
7. box _____
8. bee _____
9. platypus _____
10. ranch _____

B. Rewrite each sentence so that the underlined nouns are plural.

11. What <u>dish</u> did you try at the <u>brunch</u>?

_____

12. At the <u>circus</u> that Ira went to, he drank <u>juice</u>.

_____

13. The <u>class</u> ran out of <u>lunch</u> for their <u>picnic</u>.

_____

   Great Grammar Practice, Grade 3 © 2015 by Scholastic Teaching Resources

Name _____ Date _____

More Plural Nouns

Plural nouns name more than one person, place, or thing.

If a noun ends in a consonant and *y*, the *y* becomes *i* and *-es* is added.

baby → **babies**

If a noun ends in *f* or *fe*, the *f* or *fe* becomes *v* and *-es* is added.

half → **halves**   **wife** → **wives**

A. Write the plural form of each noun.

1. cherry _____

2. calf _____

3. elf _____

4. copy _____

5. fly _____

6. loaf _____

7. life _____

8. pony _____

9. knife _____

10. party _____

B. Rewrite each sentence so that the underlined nouns are plural.

11. Nora picked the <u>leaf</u> and the <u>berry</u>.

_____

12. From the <u>ferry</u> people could see the <u>wolf</u> on the shore.

_____

13. I think the <u>daisy</u> and the <u>poppy</u> should go on the <u>shelf</u>.

_____

 Great Grammar Practice, Grade 3 © 2015 by Scholastic Teaching Resources

Possessive Nouns

A possessive noun shows who owns something.
A singular noun ends with an apostrophe and *s*: **'s**.
A plural noun ends with *s* and an apostrophe: **s'**.

Singular Possessive Noun	Plural Possessive Noun
boy's ball	boys' ball
owner's field	owners' field

A. Rewrite each group of words so that the underlined noun is possessive. The first one is done for you.

1. the chatter of many <u>players</u>   _the players' chatter_ _____

2. the bus belonging to the <u>team</u>   _____

3. the equipment of all the <u>boys</u>   _____

4. the uniform of that <u>girl</u>   _____

5. the cheers of the <u>parents</u>   _____

B. Determine whether the underlined noun is a singular or plural possessive. Rewrite the sentence so that the possessive noun is correct.

6. This <u>organizations</u> game is an annual event.

_____

7. <u>Spectators</u> praise makes the players happy.

_____

8. <u>Mr. Satos</u> introduction was short and funny.

_____

What Is a Pronoun?

A pronoun is a word that takes the place of a noun or nouns.
Pronouns can be singular or plural.

Singular Pronouns	Plural Pronouns
I, me	we, us
you	you
he, him, she, her, it	they, them

Rita had a quilt. <u>She</u> showed <u>it</u> to Jim. <u>He</u> asked <u>her</u> many questions.

(replaces Rita)　(replaces quilt)　(replaces Jim)　(replaces Rita)

In each pair, circle the pronoun in the second sentence that
replaces the underlined noun in the first sentence.

1. The <u>quilt</u> was 100 years old.　　　　It was beautiful.

2. <u>Great-grandmother</u> made the quilt.　　She sewed for months.

3. Many <u>women</u> went to quilting bees.　　They worked together.

4. <u>Jim</u> liked the quilt.　　　　　　　　Rita told him more about quilts.

5. Old <u>quilts</u> are valuable.　　　　　　People collect them.

6. <u>Jim</u> wanted to learn more.　　　　　He went to the library.

7. <u>Jim and Rita</u> got a book about quilts.　They read the book.

8. Rita read about the <u>Friendship Basket</u>.　She learned a lot about it.

9. Jim found a picture to show <u>Rita</u>.　　He handed it to her.

10. Rita took the picture from <u>Jim</u>.　　　She thanked him.

Pronoun Places

A pronoun takes the place of a noun.

Some pronouns can be the subject of a sentence.

Never use a subject pronoun *after* an action verb.

Subject Pronouns: I you she he it we they

We visited a lighthouse. You took photos. I climbed up the tower.

(sentence subject)   (sentence subject)   (sentence subject)

A. Underline the subject pronoun in each sentence.

1. You sent a photo of the lighthouse to Vern.

2. Within minutes, he responded to the message.

3. We examined the lamp at the top of the tower.

4. It was very large and had a powerful beam.

5. Later, I described the lighthouse to Ingrid.

6. She hopes to visit this place with some friends soon.

7. They have read about other lighthouses in the area.

8. When ships sail, they can see the lighthouse beam from far away.

B. Rewrite each sentence and replace the underlined words with subject pronouns.

9. Pilar and I could see a long distance from the lighthouse.

_____

10. Pilar thought the view was stunning.

_____

Pronouns After Verbs

Certain pronouns are used after action verbs.

Pronouns After Verbs: me   you   him   her   it   us   them

Dad <u>took</u> me to a movie. The usher <u>found</u> us seats. Dad <u>thanked</u> her.

pronoun after verb   pronoun after verb   pronoun after verb

You and *it* can be used as subject pronouns and after verbs.

A. Underline the verb in each sentence. Circle the pronoun.

1. Science fiction films thrill us.

2. Dad likes them a lot.

3. Mom sometimes teases him about this interest.

4. Dad tells her all about the movie each week.

5. Mom never watches it though.

6. My brother Jay asks Dad and me about the stars.

B. Write the correct pronoun to complete each sentence.

7. Dad gives you and _____ tickets for the movies.
          I   me

8. He drives _____ to the theater.
          us   we

9. Mom joins _____ for the ride.
          he   him

10. We watch _____ drive away.
          they   them

Pronouns in Contractions

A pronoun and a verb can be combined to make a smaller word called a contraction.

An apostrophe shows where letters are left out.

Contractions

I	+ am = I'm	I	+ will = I'll
he	+ is = he's	he	+ will = he'll
she	+ is = she's	she	+ will = she'll
it	+ is = it's	it	+ will = it'll
we	+ are = we're	we	+ will = we'll
you	+ are = you're	you	+ will = you'll
they	+ are = they're	they	+ will = they'll

A. Write the two words for each contraction.

1. you're _____

2. it's _____

3. they're _____

4. we're _____

5. she'll _____

6. I'm _____

7. he'll _____

8. she's _____

B. Write a contraction in the second sentence
for the underlined words in the first sentence.

9. They will be late for lunch today. _____ miss a good meal.

10. Gil hopes you are on time.   He hopes _____ not too busy.

11. You will have fun.   _____ enjoy the lunch.

12. We are looking forward to it.   _____ pleased about this.

Review: Nouns and Pronouns

A noun is a word that names a person, place, or thing.

A pronoun is a word that takes the place of a noun or nouns.

Although the farm is small, it is a nice place to live.

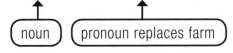

noun | pronoun replaces farm

Choose the best noun or pronoun from the word bank to complete each sentence.

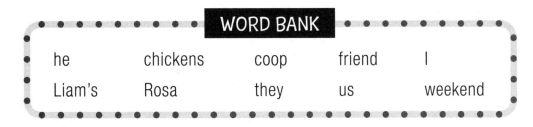

WORD BANK

| he | chickens | coop | friend | I |
| Liam's | Rosa | they | us | weekend |

1. My _____ lives on a farm.

2. His family raises _____ .

3. _____ job is to gather the eggs.

4. Sometimes, _____ also helps his brother clean

the _____ .

5. This summer, _____ hope to visit the farm.

6. Maybe _____ will invite me for a _____ .

7. My sister _____ wants to go.

8. I wonder if they will have room for both of _____ .

Name _____   Date _____

What Is a Verb?

A verb is a word that tells what someone or something does.

A verb is the main word in the predicate of a sentence.

Miss Wong's class planned a costume party.

(main verb)   (predicate tells what class did)

A. Write the verb in each sentence.

1. The students invited their families as guests. _____

2. Derek dressed as a computer. _____

3. He made the costume by himself. _____

4. He used some cardboard boxes and paint. _____

5. Miss Wong liked his costume very much. _____

B. Underline the predicate in each sentence.
Circle the verb.

6. Bonnie took a picture of Derek in his computer costume.

7. She asked him about the costume.

8. Bonnie sent the picture to the local newspaper.

9. The next day, the paper printed Bonnie's picture and a story about Derek.

10. Derek felt very proud!

Nouns and Verbs

The subject and the verb in a sentence must agree.

If the subject is a singular noun, an -s is added to the verb.

If the subject is a plural noun, the verb has no -s.

Ned builds a fire.   **The logs burn well.**

(singular subject) (-s added to verb)   (plural subject) (verb has no -s)

Write the verb that agrees with the underlined subject in each sentence.

1. The <u>flames</u> _____ the room.
   light   lights

2. Some <u>sparks</u> _____ up the fireplace.
   shoot   shoots

3. Slowly, the <u>room</u> _____ .
   warm   warms

4. The <u>temperature</u> in the room _____ .
   rise   rises

5. <u>Ned</u> _____ more logs on the fire.
   put   puts

6. <u>Ruby</u> _____ the warm, cozy room.
   enter   enters

7. <u>Shadows</u> _____ on the walls.
   dance   dances

8. The <u>heat</u> _____ Ruby and Ned sleepy.
   make   makes

9. The <u>kids</u> _____ onto the couch.
   settle   settles

10. The <u>fire</u> _____ the cold from the room.
   keep   keeps

Great Grammar Practice, Grade 3 © 2015 by Scholastic Teaching Resources

Name _____ Date _____

Verb Tenses

Verbs can tell about action in the present, past, and future.

Most past tense verbs end in *-ed*. Future verbs have *will* before them.

Present: Dogs sometimes <u>walk</u> in circles.

Past: This dog <u>walked</u> in lots of circles.

Future: He <u>will walk</u> in more circles.

Write *present*, *past*, or *future* to identify the tense of the verb in each sentence.

1. Sporty paced for hours on a rug. _____

2. The rug sits in the hall of our house. _____

3. It will wear out one day soon. _____

4. Last week, our clumsy dog tripped on the fringe of the rug. _____

5. Dad laughed at Sporty. _____

6. Now, that silly pup avoids Dad. _____

7. Maybe our pet will forgive Dad soon. _____

8. Then, they will play together again. _____

9. At the moment, Sporty looks pretty busy. _____

10. Yesterday, he circled about 50 times. _____

Name _____ Date _____

Using Verb Tenses

Verbs can tell about action in the present, past, and future.

Most past tense verbs end in -ed. Future tense verbs have *will* before them.

Present: turn
Past: turned
Future: will turn

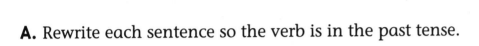

A. Rewrite each sentence so the verb is in the past tense.

1. Libby looks at the globe.

_____

2. She points to the continent of Africa.

_____

3. Cole checks out the location.

_____

B. Rewrite each sentence so that the verb is in the future tense.

4. The students write about Africa in their reports.

_____

5. Some students search for other places on the globe.

_____

6. Globes and maps help the students.

_____

Name _____ Date _____

The Verb *To Be*

The verb *to be* links the subject of a sentence to words in the rest of the sentence. It is important to use this verb correctly.

Present			Past		
I am	you are	he is	I was	you were	he was
		she is			she was
		it is			she was
we are	you are	they are	we were	you were	they were

Write the verb that agrees with the subject of each sentence.

1. I _____ the oldest in my family.
        is   am

2. The twins _____ younger than I.
            is   are

3. Kevin _____ the youngest before the baby came.
        was   were

4. Our baby _____ very cute.
            is   are

5. We _____ very proud of her.
        is   are

6. Our friends _____ excited about little Dale.
            was   were

7. You _____ good to visit us.
        is   are

8. I _____ glad that you could come.
        was   were

Name _____ Date _____

Spelling Past Tense Verbs

The past tense of most verbs ends in -ed.

For some verbs you have to change the spelling before adding -ed.

If a verb has one syllable and ends with a vowel followed by a consonant, double the final consonant before adding -ed.

   drop → **dropped**   **tag** → **tagged**

If a verb ends with e, drop the e before adding -ed.

   dance → **danced**   **bake** → **baked**

If a verb ends with a consonant and y, change the y to i before adding -ed.

   hurry → **hurried**   **worry** → **worried**

A. Circle the correct past tense spelling for each verb.

1. try	a. tried	b. tried	c. tryyed
2. zip	a. ziped	b. zipped	c. zipied
3. change	a. changeed	b. changed	c. changd
4. giggle	a. gigled	b. gigglied	c. giggled
5. bury	a. buryed	b. buried	c. burred

B. Write the past tense form of each verb.

6. stop _____ **11.** reply _____

7. copy _____ **12.** wipe _____

8. smile _____ **13.** name _____

9. grab _____ **14.** hug _____

10. cry _____ **15.** step _____

 Great Grammar Practice, Grade 3 © 2015 by Scholastic Teaching Resources

Irregular Verbs

Some verbs are irregular. They do not end in the regular way to show the past.

It is important to memorize these verbs.

Present	Past
see/sees	saw
do/does	did
know/knows	knew
draw/draws	drew
come/comes	came
write/writes	wrote
find/finds	found
bring/brings	brought

A. Rewrite each sentence using the past tense form of the verb.

1. We see a crane in March. _____

2. I quickly find my camera. _____

3. I always bring it on trips. _____

4. Mom writes down the date. _____

5. She draws pictures. _____

6. She knows a lot about birds. _____

7. The crane comes closer. _____

8. Cranes do this migration yearly. _____

B. Write sentences of your own using the past tense form of two verbs from the list above.

9. _____

10. _____

Great Grammar Practice, Grade 3 © 2015 by Scholastic Teaching Resources

More Irregular Verbs

Some verbs are irregular. They do not end in the regular way to show the past.

It is important to memorize these verbs.

Present	Past
give/gives	gave
go/goes	went
sing/sings	sang
think/thinks	thought
take/takes	took
ride/rides	rode
fly/flies	flew
begin/begins	began

A. Write *past* or *present* to identify the verb tense in each sentence.

1. A ball flies through the air. _____

2. One ball goes up, then another and another. _____

3. Mark began this activity last year. _____

4. Learning took him awhile. _____

5. I give Mark a lot of credit. _____

B. Rewrite each sentence using the past tense form of the verb.

6. Mark sings a juggling song. _____

7. Some jugglers ride unicycles. _____

8. They go around in circles. _____

9. They give us a great show. _____

 Great Grammar Practice, Grade 3 © 2015 by Scholastic Teaching Resources

Name _____ Date _____

Review: Verbs

A verb is an action word. It tells what someone or something is doing (present tense), has done (past tense), or will do (future tense). Subjects and verbs in sentences must agree.

A. Choose the best verb from the word bank to complete each sentence.

WORD BANK

was	will hurry	will take	went	were

1. We _____ so excited to get a puppy!

2. The puppy _____ to my brother when he called her.

3. Our new puppy _____ more playful than we could imagine.

4. My big sister _____ her for a walk every day.

5. They _____ if it starts to rain.

B. Rewrite each sentence so that the verb agrees with the subject.

6. The puppy were in her pen. _____

7. You was with her. _____

8. We is all there. _____

9. She are so adorable. _____

What Is an Adjective?

> An adjective is a word that describes a noun by telling what kind or how many.
>
> **Mrs. Dell made twelve jars of delicious jam.**
>   ↑   ↑
>   (how many)   (what kind)

A. Underline the two adjectives in each sentence.

1. Mrs. Dell picked the ripe berries off many bushes.

2. She put the red fruit in a large pot.

3. She spent several hours making the tasty jam.

4. Polly helped pour the jam into small, glass jars.

5. The next morning, Polly spread the jam on hot muffins.

6. She ate three muffins in five minutes!

B. Underline the adjective and circle the noun it describes in each sentence.

7. Mrs. Dell is an excellent cook.

8. She makes incredible meals in her kitchen.

9. She has taught Polly how to make wonderful dishes.

10. Polly hopes to open a popular restaurant.

11. She will invite Mrs. Dell to be an honored guest.

12. Polly will make her favorite recipe.

 Great Grammar Practice, Grade 3 © 2015 by Scholastic Teaching Resources

Name _____ Date _____

Focus on Adjectives

Adjectives can help compare two or more things.

Add *-er* when comparing two things.

Add *-est* when comparing three or more things.

Connecticut is a <u>small</u> state.

Delaware is <u>smaller</u> than Connecticut. ← two states

Rhode Island is the <u>smallest</u> state in the nation. ← three or more states

Write the *-er* and *-est* form of each adjective.

1. deep _____ _____

2. kind _____ _____

3. old _____ _____

4. light _____ _____

5. green _____ _____

6. loud _____ _____

7. short _____ _____

8. clean _____ _____

9. near _____ _____

10. wild _____ _____

11. fine _____ _____

12. dark _____ _____

Name _____ Date _____

Comparing Things

Adjectives can help compare two or more things.
Add -er when comparing two things.
Add -est when comparing three or more things.

California is a large state.

Texas is larger than California. ← two states

Alaska is the largest state in the nation. ← three or more states

Write the correct form of the adjective in each sentence.

1. It is _____ in Texas than in Maine.
warmer   warmest

2. Minnesota is _____ than Ohio.
larger   largest

3. Alaska has the _____ mountain of all states.
taller   tallest

4. Hawaii is the _____ state in the U.S.
younger   youngest

5. Where is the _____ place in the country?
cold   coldest

6. Temperatures are _____ in Arizona than North Dakota.
higher   highest

7. Georgia has a _____ climate than Montana.
milder   mildest

8. Which of all the states gets the _____ snow?
deeper   deepest

More About Adjectives

Adjectives can help compare two or more things.

For some adjectives you have to change the spelling before adding -er or -est.

If an adjective has one syllable and ends with a vowel followed by a consonant, double the final consonant before adding -er or -est.

wet → **wetter** → **wettest**

If an adjective ends with e, drop the e before adding -er or -est.

wide → **wider** → **widest**

If an adjective ends with a consonant and y, change the y to i before adding -er or -est.

dirty → **dirtier** → **dirtiest**

Write the correct forms of each adjective.

	Comparing Two Things	**Comparing Three or More Things**
1. big	_____	_____
2. fluffy	_____	_____
3. white	_____	_____
4. rocky	_____	_____
5. sleepy	_____	_____
6. thin	_____	_____
7. red	_____	_____
8. nice	_____	_____
9. safe	_____	_____
10. sad	_____	_____

Great Grammar Practice, Grade 3 © 2015 by Scholastic Teaching Resources

Name _____ Date _____

What Is an Adverb?

An adverb is a word that describes a verb.

An adverb tells when, where, or how an action happens.

When: We saw a show <u>today</u>.

Where: We saw it <u>here</u>.

How: We liked the show <u>immensely</u>.

A. The verb in each sentence is underlined. Circle the adverb that describes the verb.

1. The show <u>opened</u> yesterday.

2. We <u>read</u> the ad excitedly.

3. We <u>bought</u> tickets immediately.

4. We <u>arrived</u> early for the show.

5. The entertainer <u>appeared</u> there, too.

6. We <u>watched</u> the show happily.

B. Circle the adverb in each sentence. Write *where, when,* or *how.*

7. Now we tell our friends about the show. _____

8. They always like our suggestions. _____

9. Ollie and Eva follow us anyplace. _____

10. They quickly order tickets for themselves. _____

11. We stand nearby at the ticket booth. _____

12. Will Mavis and I see the show again? _____

Name _____ Date _____

Adverbs Ending in *-ly*

Adverbs that tell how something happens usually end in *-ly*.
Many adverbs are formed by adding *-ly* to an adjective.

Adjective	+ ly =	Adverb
sweet		sweetly
glad		gladly
light		lightly

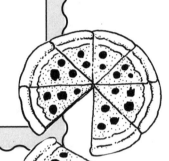

A. Underline the verb and circle the adverb in each sentence.

1. The pizza chef worked neatly at the counter.

2. He spun the dough quickly in the air.

3. He spread tomato sauce smoothly on the dough.

4. His phone rang loudly in his pocket.

5. The chef placed the pizza carefully on a chair.

6. His new assistant sat heavily on the chair by mistake!

B. Change each adjective to an adverb and use it to complete the sentence.

7. The assistant stood _____ .
slow

8. The chef looked _____ at the assistant's pants.
sharp

9. He shook his head _____ .
sad

10. The assistant left the room _____ .
quiet

 Great Grammar Practice, Grade 3 © 2015 by Scholastic Teaching Resources

Focus on Adverbs

Adverbs can help compare two or more actions.

Add *-er* when comparing two actions. Add *-est* when comparing three or more actions.	Use *more* or *most* with adverbs ending in *-ly*.
Danny stayed <u>long</u> at the party. **Mavis stayed <u>longer</u> than Danny.** **Eddie stayed <u>longest</u> of all.**	**The guests left <u>slowly</u>.** **Ella left <u>more slowly</u> than Jessie.** **The twins left <u>most slowly</u> of all.**

Write the correct forms of each adverb for making comparisons.

1. soon _____   _____

2. easily _____   _____

3. evenly _____   _____

4. clearly _____   _____

5. high _____   _____

6. hard _____   _____

7. gently _____   _____

8. late _____   _____

9. swiftly _____   _____

10. low _____   _____

Name _____ Date _____

Comparing Actions

Adverbs can help compare two or more actions.

Add *-er* when comparing two actions.
Add *-est* when comparing three or more actions.

The rain fell <u>hard</u> at noon.

The rain at noon fell <u>harder</u> than yesterday.

The rain fell <u>hardest</u> last night.

Use *more* or *most* with adverbs ending in *-ly*.

The rain fell <u>loudly</u>.

It fell <u>more loudly</u> than yesterday.

It fell <u>most loudly</u> today.

Write the correct form of the adjective in each sentence.

1. The gutters filled _____ than usual.

                           faster   more faster

2. The storm lasted _____ of any this season.

                        more longer   longest

3. The thunder boomed _____ in this storm.

                        often   more oftener

4. The lightning struck _____ than in the last storm.

                        nearer   more near

5. The clouds moved _____ than usual.

                        more slowly   most slowly

6. I watched the storm _____ than Dad did.

                        more carefully   most carefully

Name _____ Date _____

More About Adverbs

An adverb is a word that describes a verb. It tells when, where, or how and action happens.

Many adverbs are formed by adding *-ly* to an adjective. Use *more* or *most* to compare with adverbs that end in *-ly*.

Adverbs that end in *-er* compare two actions. Adverbs that end in *-est* compare three or more actions.

Read the adverbs in the word bank.
Write each of them in the correct category on the chart.

WORD BANK

anywhere	earlier	latest	perfectly	usually
away	here	lightly	strongly	warmly
carefully	inside	never	there	yesterday

When	**Where**	**How**

Great Grammar Practice, Grade 3 © 2015 by Scholastic Teaching Resources

Review: Adjectives and Adverbs

An adjective describes a noun.

An adverb describes a verb.

Penny had a large carrot.   **Penny munched happily.**

adjective   noun   verb   adverb

A. Determine whether the underlined word is a verb or a noun.
Write the adverb or adjective that describes the underlined word.

1. Penny loved _____ <u>vegetables</u>.
          fresh   freshly

2. She <u>ate</u> her carrot _____ .
                    eager   eagerly

3. _____ , a paw <u>reached</u> for Penny's carrot.
     Sudden   Suddenly

4. The _____ <u>hand</u> scared Penny.
               creepy   creepily

5. She _____ <u>snatched</u> her carrot away.
            quick   quickly

B. Determine whether the underlined word is a verb or a noun.
Circle the adverb or adjective that describes the underlined words.

6. The hairy <u>paw</u> disappeared.

7. Penny <u>looked</u> around for it.

8. She saw a furry <u>creature</u> running away.

9. Carefully, Penny <u>examined</u> her carrot.

10. She daintily <u>took</u> another bite.

Name _____ Date _____

What Is a Preposition?

A preposition is a word that can help tell where something is or when something happens.

Prepositions

above	around	behind	at
beside	by	in	into
near	on	over	to
under	with		

A. Match each word on the left to the phrase on the right that tells where in the picture that thing is.

1. chair   **a.** under the blanket

2. plane   **b.** beside the trash can

3. bear   **c.** near the desk

4. sneaker   **d.** above the bed

B. Circle the preposition in each sentence.

5. The cat sits by the window.

6. The pillow is behind the bear.

7. The lamp is on the desk.

8. The dog sleeps under the bed.

Name _____ Date _____

Building Sentences With Prepositions

A preposition is a word that can help tell where something is or when something happens. You can build sentences by adding phrases beginning with a preposition.

Toby liked camping.

Toby liked camping <u>in the summer.</u>

when Toby liked camping

Prepositional Phrases

after one week

in his arms

up a big hill

under the stars

to the mountains

into the tent

at dawn

near a creek

Choose the best phrase from the list above to build each sentence. Use each phrase only once.

1. Last weekend Toby went _____ .

2. His family left home _____ .

3. They found a campsite _____ .

4. Toby helped carry supplies _____ .

5. His Mom put them _____ .

6. They all went for a hike _____ .

7. Toby and Dad slept _____ .

8. They were ready to leave _____ .

 Great Grammar Practice, Grade 3 © 2015 by Scholastic Teaching Resources

Name _____ Date _____

Review: Prepositions

A preposition is a word that can help tell where something is or when something happens.

WORD BANK

above	beside
along	from
in	on
over	toward
within	at

Choose the best preposition from the word bank to complete each sentence. Use each word only once.

1. It was a hot day and the sun was high _____ the sky.

2. Kady's sunglasses protected her eyes _____ the sun.

3. She relaxed _____ her beach chair.

4. She had a cold beverage

   _____ her reach.

5. There were swaying palm trees

   _____ the water's edge.

6. The radio _____ the chair played her favorite songs.

7. Just then, _____ her shoulder, she noticed a beachball.

8. It was coming _____ her quickly!

9. She reached her hands _____ her head.

10. Kady caught it _____ the last second!

Name _____ Date _____

Capitals in Titles

The titles of books begin with capital letters.
Capitalize first, last, and important words in titles.
Underline titles that you write. Use italics on a computer.

<u>A Wrinkle in Time</u>   *A Wrinkle in Time*

A. Write these titles correctly. Remember to underline them.

1. the mouse and the motorcycle _____

2. nate the great _____

3. tuck everlasting _____

4. george and martha _____

5. be nice to spiders _____

B. Rewrite the sentences correctly. Remember to underline the titles.

6. when I was nine is by james stevenson.

_____

7. jerry spinelli wrote third grade angels.

_____

8. winter of the ice wizard is a book by mary pope osborne.

_____

9. jeff kinney wrote diary of a wimpy kid.

_____

Name _____   Date _____

More About Capitals

A title before someone's name begins with a capital letter.
Most titles are abbreviated and end with a period.
When you write an initial, use a capital letter and period.

Titles: Mrs.   Mr.   Ms.   Miss   Dr.

Initials: B. P. Perlman   B. P. P.

A. Write each name and title correctly.

1. dr anna rodriguez   _____

2. mr and mrs clark   _____

3. y l okimoto   _____

4. miss helen j nichols   _____

5. ms molly jackson   _____

B. Rewrite the sentences correctly.

6. dr seuss was born on march 2

_____

7. miss susan b anthony was born on february 15

_____

8. e b white wrote charlotte's web in 1952

_____

9. j k rowling published harry potter and the sorcerer's stone in 1997

_____

Name _____ Date _____

Commas in Addresses

Commas separate the name of a city and a state.
Abbreviations for states are in capital letters.

Columbus, Ohio   **Houston, TX**

city   state   city   abbreviation for state

Write the cities and states correctly.

1. billings montana _____

2. georgetown md _____

3. paducah kentucky _____

4. tucson az _____

5. orlando fl _____

6. barre vermont _____

7. san diego ca _____

8. boise idaho _____

9. langley washington _____

10. traverse city mi _____

11. chicago il _____

12. athens georgia _____

Name _____   Date _____

Commas in a Series

Commas separate three or more words or phrases in a series.

Mom had a hat, scarf, gloves, and purse.

commas separate words in series

Rewrite each sentence using commas to separate words in a series.

1. The children are named Kevin Kayla and Kyle.

_____

2. Their cat likes to eat play and sleep.

_____

3. There are shirts pants socks and books in the suitcase.

_____

4. Kevin can ride a skateboard a bicycle and a scooter.

_____

5. The dog wants to bury the bone in the flower bed under the bush or behind the tree.

_____

_____

Quotation Marks and Commas

Quotation marks show the exact words that someone says.

A comma separates the speaker's words from the rest of the sentence.

Kito said, "I forgot my lines."   **Fay told her, "Don't worry."**

quotation marks show Kito's exact words

comma separates Fay's words from rest of the sentence

You're stepping on my costume.

I am so nervous!

Are those lights too bright?

The orchestra is warming up.

Is everyone ready?

Is the audience out there yet?

Your make up is perfect.

I'll move that set.

Write quotations from the speech balloons to complete the sentences below.
Use each quotation only once.

1. The conductor said _____

2. Said the stagehand _____

3. Lea inquired _____

4. Asked the electrician _____

5. The director asked _____

6. Peter complained to Bud _____

7. The makeup artist said _____

8. Paula admitted _____

Name _____ Date _____

Writing Dialogue

Quotation marks show the exact words that someone says.

If the quotation comes first, a comma, question mark, or exclamation mark separates the speaker's words from the rest of the sentence.

A capital letter begins the first word of a quotation.

"I like that scarf," said Deena.   "Thank you!" exclaimed Kenji.

| exact words of Deena | | capital letter | exclamation mark |

Rewrite each sentence correctly.

1. Deena asked what color is the wool

_____

2. the color is sort of heather answered Kenji

_____

3. Molly said my mother sometimes dyes her own wool

_____

4. Deena exclaimed that is really cool

_____

5. would your mom make a scarf for me asked Deena

_____

6. let's learn how to knit so we can make our own scarves suggested Molly

_____

Name _____ Date _____

Review: Capitalization and Punctuation

Using capitals and correct punctuation makes a sentence easier to read. Remember to use capitals at the beginning of sentences and proper nouns.

A. Rewrite the sentences correctly.

1. chris van allsburg was born in grand rapids michigan

_____

2. jane yolen is from new york new york

_____

3. the hometown of julius lester is st louis missouri

_____

4. steven kellogg was born in norwalk connecticut

_____

5. the birthplace of joanna cole is newark new jersey

_____

B. Write a question that needs commas to separate words in a series.

6. _____

_____

Name _____ Date _____

Word Families

Some words can be grouped into families because they have the same spelling base.

-art	-ear	-ound	-ark
art	ear	bound	ark
cart	clear	bound	bark
dart	dear	ground	mark

A. Add the letters to form words in the word families *-art, -ear, -ound,* and *-ark.*

1. t + ear = _____

2. h + ear = _____

3. m + ound = _____

4. st + art = _____

5. p + ark = _____

6. s + ound = _____

7. ch + art = _____

8. gr + ound = _____

9. g + ear = _____

10. sm + art = _____

B. Write two words in the same word family as each word below. Use a dictionary for help.

11. night _____ _____

12. took _____ _____

13. sing _____ _____

14. rind _____ _____

15. bank _____ _____

16. clown _____ _____

Great Grammar Practice, Grade 3 © 2015 by Scholastic Teaching Resources

Words With *ch*, *sh*, and *th*

Some words begin or end with the consonant sound /ch/, /sh/ or /th/.

Beginning Sound		End Punctuation	
chap	chin	much	coach
show	shape	hush	wash
thing	thank	with	path

A. Write a word that begins or ends with *sh*, *ch*, or *th* for each picture.

1. _____

2. _____

3. _____

4. _____

5. _____

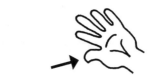

6. _____

B. Add *sh*, *ch,* or *th* to make new words.

7. _____ ew   **10.** _____ ought

8. su _____   **11.** bru _____

9. _____ ack   **12.** bo _____

Name _____ Date _____

What Is a Prefix?

A prefix is a group of letters at the beginning of a word that changes the word's meaning.

Word	Prefix and Meaning	New Word
view	*pre-* meaning "before"	preview
happy	*un-* meaning "not"	unhappy

A. Add the prefix *pre-* to make new words.

1. pre + school = _____   **4.** pre + paid   = _____

2. pre + cook   = _____   **5.** pre + heat   = _____

3. pre + test   = _____   **6.** pre + historic = _____

B. Add the prefix *un-* to make new words.

7. un + lucky = _____   **10.** un + lock   = _____

8. un + fair   = _____   **11.** un + kind   = _____

9. un + usual = _____   **12.** un + true   = _____

C. Complete each sentence with a word that has the prefix *un-* or *pre-*. Use a dictionary to help you.

13. If something is too difficult, you may be _____ to do it.

14. Mom will _____ the crust before she bakes the pie.

Great Grammar Practice, Grade 3 © 2015 by Scholastic Teaching Resources

What Is a Suffix?

A suffix is a group of letters at the end of a word that changes the word's meaning.

A suffix also changes the word from one part of speech to another.

Word	Part of Speech	Suffix and Meaning	New Word	Part of Speech
catch	verb	*-er* meaning "a person who"	catcher	noun
cheer	noun	*-ful* meaning "full of"	cheerful	adjective

A. Add the suffix *-er* to make new words.

1. jump + er = _____

2. sweep + er = _____

3. work + er = _____

4. paint + er = _____

5. teach + er = _____

6. clean + er = _____

B. Add the suffix *-ful* to make new words.

7. harm + ful = _____

8. dread + ful = _____

9. peace + ful = _____

10. success + ful = _____

11. color + ful = _____

12. grace + ful = _____

C. Complete each sentence with a word that has the suffix *-er* or *-ful*. Use a dictionary to help you.

13. Someone who is full of thanks is _____.

14. If you play well, you are a good _____.

Name _____ Date _____

Review: Spelling

Many words include spelling clues that can help you learn more words.

These clues include different letter combinations that begin or end words, such as *ch*, *sh*, or *th*. They also include word families, prefixes, and suffixes.

A. Complete the sentences below with a word that begins or ends with *ch*, *sh*, or *th*. Use a dictionary to help you.

1. We polished our shoes to make them _____ .

2. The young _____ grew one _____

   in the last six months.

3. My sister and brother _____ asked me to

   _____ their swing.

4. Each night to get clean, I can either take a _____ or a

   _____ .

B. Complete the sentences below with a word that begins with the prefix *un-* or *pre-*, or ends with the suffix *-er* or *-ful*. Use a dictionary to help you.

5. When I put away the dishes, my mom said I was _____ .

6. Before we read the book, we will _____ the chapter titles.

7. After vacation, we must _____ our suitcases.

8. I was in the back row, but I could clearly hear the voice of the opera

   _____ .

Great Grammar Practice, Grade 3 © 2015 by Scholastic Teaching Resources

Activity 1: A. 1. statement 2. statement 3. question 4. statement 5. question 6. question 7. statement 8. statement B. 9.–10. Answers will vary. Check that students write complete sentences.

Activity 2: A. 1. Mini 2. The spoon 3. The table 4. Dad 5. The cake 6. Mom B. 7. The cake 8. Dad 9. Mini 10. The family

Activity 3: A. 1. Sara; wears 2. A bike; has 3. A scooter; lacks 4. Ken; pushes 5. The friends; race 6. They; meet B. 7. ride on bike paths 8. rings her bell 9.–10. Order may vary. 9. looks at his watch 10. calls to Sara

Activity 4: A. 1. statement 2. command 3. command 4. command 5. statement B. 6. exclamation 7. command 8. command 9. exclamation 10. command

Activity 5: 1. statement 2. question 3. statement 4. exclamation 5. command 6. statement 7. exclamation 8. question 9. question 10. command

Activity 6: 1. Jeb studied hard for the test. 2. Was he well prepared for all the questions? 3. Look at his grade. 4. Fantastic! 5. Keep up the good work. 6. Jeb, what is your favorite subject?

Activity 7: 1. but 2. and 3. or 4. but 5. or 6. and 7. but 8. and 9. or

Activity 8: A. 1. **before** it broke 2. **because** Luna ran into the table 3. **after** Luna had this accident 4. **because** we used the table a lot 5. **since** he is a good worker B. 6. dependent clause 7. sentence 8. dependent clause 9. dependent clause 10. sentence

Activity 9: 1. while 2. after 3. although 4. because or since 5. because or since 6. before 7. until 8. than

Activity 10: A. 1. statement 2. question 3. command 4. exclamation 5. question B. 6. **Our grandmother** meets us every Sunday. 7. **She** likes to take us to the museum. 8. **My sister and I** enjoy looking at paintings. 9. **We** paint our own pictures when we get home. 10. **Grandma** thinks we are great artists!

Activity 11: A. 1. trees; house 2. Squirrels; chipmunks; animals; forest 3. day; bear; clearing; cabin 4. family; window 5. pioneer; neighbor B. Answers will vary. Possible: 6. pioneer; family; trees 7. barn; animals 8. neighbors; town 9. women; dinner; the workers 10. time

Activity 12: A. 1. friends, dinner; Peter, Tuesday 2. group; First Wok, Mulberry Street 3. chef, restaurant; Jodi 4. train; Hector, Anna, Falls Village 5. way, station; Mountain View School 6. Lake Erie 7. common noun 8. Flag Day 9. Europe 10. common noun 11. Sunday 12. common noun

Activity 13: A. 1. contentment 2. pleasure 3. pureness 4. love 5. brotherhood 6. gentleness 7. beauty 8. joy B. 9.–10. Sentences will vary. Check that students use the abstract nouns correctly.

Activity 14: A. 1. brushes 2. passes 3. bunches 4. faxes 5. guesses 6. plants 7. boxes 8. bees 9. platypuses 10. ranches B. 11. What dishes did you try at the brunches? 12. At the circuses that Ira went to, he drank juices. 13. The classes ran out of lunches for their picnics.

Activity 15: A. 1. cherries 2. calves 3. elves 4. copies 5. flies 6. loaves 7. lives 8. ponies 9. knives 10. parties B. 11. Nora picked the leaves and the berries. 12. From the ferries people could see the wolves on the shore. 13. I think the daisies and the poppies should go on the shelves.

Activity 16: A. 1. the players' chatter 2. the team's bus 3. the boys' equipment 4. the girl's uniform 5. the parents' cheers B. 6. This organization's game is an annual event. 7. Spectators' praise makes the players happy. 8. Mr. Sato's introduction was short and funny.

Activity 17: A. 1. It 2. She 3. They 4. him 5. them 6. He B. 7. They 8. it 9. her 10. him

Activity 18: A. 1. You 2. He 3. We 4. It 5. I 6. She 7. They 8. they B. 9. We could see a long distance from the lighthouse. 10. She thought the view was stunning.

Activity 19: A. 1. thrill; us 2. likes; them 3. teases; him 4. tells; her 5. watches; it 6. asks; me B. 7. me 8. us 9. him 10. them

Activity 20: A. 1. you are 2. it is 3. they are 4. we are 5 she will 6. I am 7. he will 8. she is B. 9. They'll 10. you're 11. You'll 12. We're

Activity 21: 1. friend 2. chickens 3. Liam's 4. he; coop 5. I 6. they; weekend 7. Rosa 8. us

Activity 22: A. 1. invited 2. dressed 3. made 4. used 5. liked B. 6. **took** a picture of Derek in his computer costume 7. **asked** him about the costumes 8. **sent** the picture to the local newspaper 9. **printed** Bonnie's picture and a story about Derek 10. **felt** very proud

Activity 23: A. 1. light 2. shoot 3. warms 4. rises 5. puts B. 6. enters 7. dance 8. makes 9. settle 10. keeps

Activity 24: 1. past 2. present 3. future 4. past 5. past 6. present 7. future 8. future 9. present 10. past

Activity 25: A. 1. Libby looked at the globe. 2. She pointed to the continent of Africa. 3. Cole checked out the location. B. 4. The students will write about Africa in their reports. 5. Some students will search for other places on the globe. 6. Globes and maps will help the students.

Activity 26: 1. am 2. are 3. was 4. is 5. are 6. were 7. are 8. was

Activity 27: A. 1. a 2. b 3. b 4. c 5. b B. 6. stopped 7. copied 8. smiled 9. grabbed 10. cried 11. replied 12. wiped 13. named 14. hugged 15. stepped

Activity 28: A. 1. We saw a crane in March. 2. I quickly found my camera. 3. I always brought it on trips. 4. Mom wrote down the date. 5. She drew pictures. 6. She knew a lot about birds. 7. The crane came closer. 8. Cranes did this migration yearly. B. 9.–10. Answers will vary. Check that students use the past tense verb correctly.

Activity 29: A. 1. present 2. present 3. past 4. past 5. present B. 6. Mark sang a juggling song. 7. Some jugglers rode unicycles. 8. They went around in circles. 9. They gave us a great show.

Activity 30: A. 1. were 2. went 3. was 4. will take 5. will hurry B. 6. The puppy was in her pen. 7. You were with her. 8. We are all there. 9 She is so adorable.

Activity 31: A. 1. ripe; many 2. red; large 3. several; tasty 4. small; glass 5. next; hot 6. three; five B. 7. excellent; cook 8. incredible; meals 9. wonderful; dishes 10. popular; restaurant 11. honored; guest 12. favorite; recipe

Activity 32: 1. deeper; deepest 2. kinder; kindest 3. older; oldest 4. lighter; lightest 5. greener; greenest 6. louder; loudest 7. shorter; shortest 8. cleaner; cleanest 9. nearer; nearest 10. wilder; wildest 11. finer; finest 12. darker; darkest

Activity 33: 1. warmer 2. larger 3. tallest 4. youngest 5. coldest 6. higher 7. milder 8. deepest

Activity 34: 1. bigger; biggest 2. fluffier; fluffiest 3. whiter; whitest 4. rockier; rockiest, 5. sleepier; sleepiest 6. thinner; thinnest 7. redder; reddest 8. nicer; nicest 9. safer; safest 10. sadder; saddest

Activity 35: A. 1. yesterday 2. excitedly 3. immediately 4. early 5. there 6. happily B. 7. Now; when 8. always; when 9. anyplace; where 10. quickly; how 11. nearby; where 12. again; when

Activity 36: A. 1. worked; neatly 2. spun; quickly 3. spread; smoothly 4. rang; loudly 5. placed; carefully 6. sat; heavily B. 7. slowly 8. sharply 9. sadly 10. quietly